Table Of Contents

Chapter 1: Introduction to Remote Project Management

What is Remote Project Management?

Remote project management is the practice of overseeing and guiding a project team from a distance, using various tools and technologies to communicate and collaborate effectively. In today's fast-paced and globalized world, the need for remote project management has become increasingly common as teams are often spread out across different locations and time zones.

One of the key aspects of remote project management is the use of technology to facilitate communication and collaboration. This can include video conferencing, project management software, instant messaging, and other tools that allow team members to stay connected and work together seamlessly. By leveraging these tools, project managers can ensure that everyone is on the same page and working towards the same goals, even if they are not physically in the same location.

Another important aspect of remote project management is the need for strong leadership and organization skills. Project managers must be able to set clear goals and expectations, delegate tasks effectively, and provide guidance and support to team members, even when they are not in the same physical space. This requires excellent communication skills, as well as the ability to adapt to different working styles and preferences.

Overall, remote project management offers many benefits, including increased flexibility, access to a larger talent pool, and cost savings. However, it also comes with its own unique challenges, such as the potential for miscommunication, cultural differences, and time zone differences. By understanding these challenges and implementing best practices for remote project management, project managers can ensure that their teams are successful and productive, no matter where they are located.

Benefits of Remote Project Management

Remote project management offers numerous benefits to both project managers and programme managers. In this subchapter, we will explore some of the key advantages of adopting remote project management practices.

One of the most significant benefits of remote project management is increased flexibility. By allowing team members to work from anywhere, project managers can tap into a global talent pool and assemble teams based on skills and expertise rather than geographical location. This flexibility also extends to project managers themselves, who can work from home or other remote locations, saving time and money on commuting.

Remote project management also promotes better work-life balance. With the ability to work from anywhere, team members can better manage their personal obligations and schedules, leading to increased job satisfaction and productivity. Programme managers can also benefit from this flexibility, as they can oversee multiple projects without the need to be physically present in each location. Another key advantage of remote project management is cost savings. By eliminating the need for a physical office space, project managers can significantly reduce overhead costs. Additionally, remote project management allows for more efficient use of resources, as team members can work on multiple projects simultaneously without the need for travel.

Finally, remote project management promotes better communication and collaboration. With the use of technology tools such as video conferencing, project managers can easily connect with team members and stakeholders regardless of their location. This leads to increased transparency, accountability, and overall project success.

In conclusion, remote project management offers a wide range of benefits for project managers, programme managers, and their teams. By embracing remote work practices, project managers can improve flexibility, work-life balance, cost savings, and communication, ultimately leading to more effective project management.

In the rapidly evolving world of project management, remote project management has become increasingly common. With the rise of technology and global connectivity, project managers are often tasked with overseeing projects and teams that are scattered across different locations. While remote project management offers numerous benefits, it also presents its fair share of challenges.

One of the biggest challenges of remote project management is communication. In a traditional office setting, project managers can easily walk over to team members' desks to discuss project updates, address concerns, and provide feedback. However, when team members are spread out across different locations, communication becomes more complicated. Project managers must rely on email, phone calls, video conferencing, and other tools to keep the lines of communication open. Misunderstandings can easily occur in the absence of face-to-face interactions, leading to delays and confusion.

Another challenge of remote project management is team collaboration. In a remote setting, team members may feel isolated and disconnected from their colleagues. Building a sense of camaraderie and teamwork can be more challenging when team members are not physically present in the same location. Project managers must find ways to foster collaboration and create a sense of unity among team members, even when they are miles apart.

Additionally, remote project management requires project managers to be more flexible and adaptable. With team members working in different time zones and with varying schedules, project managers must be able to accommodate different working styles and preferences. This can be challenging, especially when trying to coordinate meetings and deadlines across different locations. Overall, remote project management presents unique challenges that require project managers to be creative, resourceful, and proactive in finding solutions. By being aware of these challenges and implementing strategies to overcome them, project managers can successfully lead remote teams and achieve project success.

Chapter 2: Setting Up Your Remote Project Team

Building a Strong Remote Team

In today's increasingly digital world, remote work has become more prevalent than ever before. As a project or programme manager, it is crucial to understand how to build a strong remote team in order to ensure the success of your projects. This subchapter will provide you with valuable insights and tools to effectively manage your remote team and achieve your project goals.

One of the key components of building a strong remote team is effective communication. Without the ability to easily communicate with your team members, it can be challenging to keep everyone on the same page and working towards a common goal. Utilizing tools such as video conferencing, instant messaging, and project management software can help facilitate communication and collaboration among team members, regardless of their physical location.

In addition to communication, it is important to establish clear goals and expectations for your remote team. Setting clear deadlines, deliverables, and performance metrics can help keep your team members motivated and focused on achieving their objectives. Regular check-ins and progress updates can also help ensure that everyone is on track and working towards the desired outcomes. Building trust among team members is another essential aspect of creating a strong remote team. Trust is the foundation of any successful team, and it is especially important when team members are not physically present in the same location. Encouraging open and honest communication, recognizing individual contributions, and fostering a sense of camaraderie can help build trust and strengthen the bond among team members.

By following the strategies outlined in this subchapter, you can effectively build a strong remote team that is capable of achieving your project goals. With the right tools and techniques, remote project management can be made easy, allowing you to successfully lead your team to success, regardless of their physical location.

Defining Roles and Responsibilities

Defining roles and responsibilities is a crucial aspect of effective remote project management. In order to ensure the success of a project, it is essential for project managers and programme managers to clearly outline the roles and responsibilities of each team member. One of the key challenges of remote project management is the lack of face-to-face interaction, which can lead to miscommunication and confusion about who is responsible for what. By defining roles and responsibilities from the outset, project managers can avoid these pitfalls and set their teams up for success.

When defining roles and responsibilities, it is important to consider the skills and expertise of each team member. Assign tasks based on individual strengths and capabilities, and ensure that everyone understands their role within the project.

Communication is also key when defining roles and responsibilities in a remote setting. Make sure that team members are aware of who is responsible for what, and encourage open communication to address any issues or concerns that may arise.

Additionally, it is important to regularly review and update roles and responsibilities as the project progresses. As priorities shift and new challenges emerge, it may be necessary to adjust the roles and responsibilities of team members to ensure that the project stays on track.

By clearly defining roles and responsibilities, project managers and programme managers can foster a sense of accountability and ownership among team members, leading to a more efficient and successful project. In the fast-paced world of remote project management, having a solid foundation of well-defined roles and responsibilities is essential for driving results and achieving project goals.

Communication Strategies for Remote Teams

Communication is the key to success for any team, but it becomes even more crucial when managing a remote team. In this subchapter, we will discuss some effective communication strategies for remote teams that will help project managers and programme managers ensure smooth operations and successful project delivery.

One of the first things to consider when managing a remote team is setting up clear communication channels. Utilize tools such as video conferencing, instant messaging, and project management software to keep everyone connected and informed. Regular check-ins and team meetings are essential to keep everyone on the same page and address any issues that may arise.

Another important strategy is to encourage open and transparent communication among team members. Encourage team members to share their ideas, concerns, and feedback openly to foster a collaborative environment. This will help build trust among team members and improve overall team dynamics.

It is also important to establish clear communication protocols and guidelines for remote teams. Set expectations for response times, meeting schedules, and communication etiquette to ensure smooth and efficient communication. Create a communication plan that outlines how and when team members should communicate with each other and with stakeholders.

Lastly, don't underestimate the power of non-verbal communication in remote teams. Use video calls whenever possible to facilitate face-to-face interactions and build stronger relationships among team members. Emphasize the importance of active listening and empathy to ensure that everyone feels heard and understood.

By implementing these communication strategies, project managers and programme managers can effectively manage their remote teams and achieve project success. Communication is the lifeline of remote teams, so invest time and effort into developing strong communication practices to ensure the success of your remote projects.

Chapter 3: Tools for Remote Project Management

Project Management Software

Project management software has become an essential tool for remote project managers looking to effectively manage their teams and projects. With the rise of remote work, having the right software in place can make all the difference in ensuring that projects are completed on time and within budget.

There are many different project management software options available, each offering its own unique features and benefits. From task tracking and team collaboration to budgeting and reporting, these tools can help streamline the project management process and keep teams organized and on track.

One popular project management software option is Trello, which allows users to create boards, lists, and cards to track tasks and progress. With features like due dates, checklists, and attachments, Trello makes it easy for remote project managers to stay organized and keep everyone on the same page.

Another popular choice is Asana, which offers a more robust set of features for larger and more complex projects. With tools for project planning, task management, and team communication, Asana is a great option for remote project managers looking to streamline their workflows and improve collaboration.

No matter which project management software you choose, the key is to find a tool that fits the specific needs of your team and project. By investing in the right software and taking the time to learn how to use it effectively, remote project managers can set themselves up for success and ensure that their projects are completed efficiently and successfully.

Collaboration Tools

In today's fast-paced and globalized world, remote project management has become increasingly common. As project managers and programme managers, it is essential to have the right tools at your disposal to effectively manage your projects from a distance. Collaboration tools are a key component of successful remote project management, enabling teams to communicate, collaborate, and stay organized no matter where they are located.

One of the most popular collaboration tools for remote project managers is project management software. These platforms allow you to create and track tasks, set deadlines, assign team members, and monitor progress in real-time. With features such as Gantt charts, Kanban boards, and customizable dashboards, project management software makes it easy to keep your projects on track and your team aligned.

Another essential collaboration tool for remote project managers is video conferencing software. Platforms like Zoom, Microsoft Teams, and Google Meet allow team members to connect face-to-face, regardless of their physical location. Video conferencing is invaluable for holding team meetings, conducting project updates, and building rapport among team members.

In addition to project management and video conferencing tools, document sharing platforms are also essential for remote project managers. Tools like Google Drive, Dropbox, and Microsoft OneDrive allow team members to collaborate on documents, spreadsheets, and presentations in real-time. These platforms ensure that everyone is working from the most up-to-date information and minimize the risk of version control issues.

By leveraging collaboration tools effectively, remote project managers can overcome the challenges of managing projects from a distance and ensure the success of their teams. Investing in the right tools and training your team to use them effectively will set you up for success in the world of remote project management.

Time Tracking and Productivity Tools

As a project or programme manager in the remote work environment, one of the biggest challenges you may face is tracking time and ensuring productivity among your team members. Luckily, there are a variety of tools available to help you streamline this process and keep your projects on track.

Time tracking tools such as Toggl, Harvest, and Clockify can help you and your team members log hours worked on specific tasks and projects. These tools not only help you keep track of billable hours but also provide valuable insights into where time is being spent and how it can be better allocated for maximum efficiency.

Additionally, productivity tools like Asana, Trello, and Monday.com can help you organize tasks, set deadlines, and track progress on various projects. These tools allow for easy collaboration among team members, even when working remotely, and provide a centralized hub for all project-related information.

By utilizing time tracking and productivity tools, remote project managers can better monitor team performance, identify areas for improvement, and ensure that deadlines are met. These tools can also help project managers allocate resources effectively, prioritize tasks, and communicate expectations clearly to team members.

In the fast-paced world of remote project management, time tracking and productivity tools are essential for staying organized, efficient, and on schedule. By incorporating these tools into your management strategy, you can increase productivity, improve communication, and ultimately achieve greater success in your projects.

Chapter 4: Effective Communication in Remote Project Management

Establishing Communication Protocols

Establishing effective communication protocols is crucial for successful remote project management. Without clear communication channels in place, team members can feel disconnected, leading to misunderstandings, delays, and ultimately, project failure. In this subchapter, we will explore the key steps to establishing communication protocols that will help keep your remote team on track and working efficiently.

The first step in establishing communication protocols is to define the preferred communication methods for your team. This could include email, video conferencing, instant messaging, or project management tools. By setting clear guidelines on how and when team members should communicate, you can ensure that everyone is on the same page and working towards common goals.

Next, it is important to establish regular check-in meetings to keep everyone updated on project progress, address any issues, and ensure that tasks are being completed on time. These meetings can be conducted via video conferencing or phone calls, depending on the preferences of your team members.

In addition to regular check-ins, it is also important to encourage open communication among team members. This means creating a safe space for team members to ask questions, raise concerns, and provide feedback. By fostering an environment of trust and transparency, you can help prevent misunderstandings and foster collaboration among team members.

Finally, it is important to document all communication protocols and make them easily accessible to team members. This could include creating a communication plan that outlines the preferred methods of communication, meeting schedules, and guidelines for resolving conflicts. By having these protocols in writing, you can ensure that everyone is aware of expectations and responsibilities when it comes to communication.

By following these steps and establishing clear communication protocols, you can help keep your remote team organized, motivated, and working towards project success.

Overcoming Communication Barriers

In the fast-paced world of remote project management, communication is key. However, managing teams and projects from afar can present unique challenges when it comes to effective communication. In this subchapter, we will explore strategies and tools to help project managers overcome communication barriers in remote project management.

One of the biggest challenges in remote project management is the lack of face-to-face communication. Without the ability to read body language or pick up on nonverbal cues, misunderstandings can easily occur. To overcome this barrier, project managers must be proactive in establishing clear communication channels. This can include regular video calls, instant messaging platforms, and project management tools that allow for real-time collaboration.

Another common communication barrier in remote project management is the difference in time zones. When team members are spread out across the globe, coordinating meetings and deadlines can be a logistical nightmare. To address this challenge, project managers should establish a clear communication schedule that takes into account the different time zones of team members. This may involve rotating meeting times to accommodate different regions or setting expectations around response times for emails and messages. Additionally, cultural differences can also impact communication in remote project management. Different cultures may have varying communication styles, norms, and expectations. To overcome this barrier, project managers should take the time to understand the cultural backgrounds of their team members and adapt their communication strategies accordingly. This may involve being more explicit in instructions, avoiding slang or idioms that may not translate well, and being mindful of different communication preferences.

By being proactive, flexible, and culturally sensitive, project managers can overcome communication barriers in remote project management and ensure that their teams are set up for success. With the right strategies and tools in place, effective communication is within reach for remote project managers.

Remote Team Meetings and Updates

In the world of remote project management, team meetings and regular updates are vital for keeping everyone on the same page and ensuring that tasks are completed efficiently and effectively. With team members spread out across different locations and time zones, it can be challenging to coordinate meetings and provide updates in a timely manner. However, with the right tools and strategies in place, remote team meetings and updates can be streamlined and productive.

One of the key tools for remote team meetings is video conferencing software. Platforms such as Zoom, Microsoft Teams, and Google Meet allow project managers to hold virtual meetings with their team members, enabling face-to-face communication even when team members are miles apart. These tools also allow for screen sharing, file sharing, and chat features, making it easy to collaborate and share information during meetings.

In addition to video conferencing, project managers can also utilize project management software to provide updates and track progress on tasks. Platforms such as Asana, Trello, and Jira allow team members to see what tasks they are responsible for, monitor deadlines, and communicate with team members in real-time. This ensures that everyone is aware of their responsibilities and can easily track the progress of the project.

When scheduling remote team meetings, it is important to consider the time zones of all team members to ensure that everyone can attend. It may be necessary to rotate meeting times to accommodate different time zones, or to record meetings for team members who are unable to attend live.

Overall, remote team meetings and updates are essential for successful project management in a remote setting. By utilizing the right tools and strategies, project managers can keep their team members engaged and informed, leading to increased productivity and successful project outcomes.

Chapter 5: Managing Remote Project Risks

Identifying Risks in Remote Projects

One of the key challenges of remote project management is the ability to identify and mitigate risks effectively. Without the luxury of face-to-face interactions and real-time monitoring, project managers must rely on other tools and techniques to identify potential risks that could derail their projects.

One of the first steps in identifying risks in remote projects is to conduct a thorough risk assessment. This involves analyzing the project scope, objectives, and constraints to identify potential threats and opportunities. By understanding the project environment and stakeholders, project managers can better anticipate and plan for potential risks.

In remote projects, communication is essential for identifying risks. Project managers must establish clear channels of communication with team members, stakeholders, and other project partners to ensure that any potential risks are identified and addressed in a timely manner. Regular check-ins, status updates, and progress reports can help project managers stay informed about the project's status and identify any emerging risks.

Another important aspect of identifying risks in remote projects is leveraging technology and tools. Project managers can use project management software, collaboration platforms, and other tools to track progress, monitor performance, and identify potential risks. By using these tools effectively, project managers can gain valuable insights into the project's health and identify any potential risks before they escalate.

In conclusion, identifying risks in remote projects requires a combination of thorough risk assessment, effective communication, and the use of technology and tools. By following these best practices, project managers can better anticipate and mitigate risks in their remote projects, ultimately leading to more successful outcomes.

Mitigating Risks in Remote Projects

Remote project management poses unique challenges that can increase the likelihood of risks derailing the project. However, with the right strategies in place, project managers can effectively mitigate these risks and ensure successful project delivery. In this subchapter, we will explore key tactics for mitigating risks in remote projects and provide practical tools for effective risk management.

One of the first steps in mitigating risks in remote projects is to conduct a thorough risk assessment. This involves identifying potential risks, assessing their likelihood and impact, and developing a risk management plan. By proactively identifying risks, project managers can implement strategies to prevent or minimize their impact on the project.

Communication is essential in remote project management, especially when it comes to risk mitigation. Project managers must establish clear lines of communication with team members, stakeholders, and vendors to ensure that everyone is aware of potential risks and their respective mitigation strategies. Regular check-ins, status updates, and virtual meetings can help keep everyone on the same page and facilitate quick decision-making in the event of a risk eventuating.

Another important aspect of mitigating risks in remote projects is the use of technology and tools. Project managers can leverage project management software, collaboration platforms, and communication tools to streamline project workflows, track progress, and monitor risks in real-time. These tools can also help project managers identify warning signs of potential risks and take proactive measures to address them before they escalate.

By following these strategies and utilizing the right tools, project managers can effectively mitigate risks in remote projects and increase the likelihood of project success. Ultimately, proactive risk management is essential for remote project managers to navigate the unique challenges of remote work and deliver projects on time and within budget.

Contingency Planning for Remote Projects

In today's fast-paced and globalized world, remote project management has become increasingly common. With teams spread across different time zones and locations, project managers face unique challenges that require careful planning and preparation. One of the key aspects of successful remote project management is contingency planning.

Contingency planning involves anticipating potential risks and developing strategies to mitigate them. In the context of remote projects, this is especially important as there are additional factors to consider, such as communication barriers and technical issues. By having a solid contingency plan in place, project managers can ensure that their projects stay on track, even in the face of unexpected challenges.

One of the first steps in contingency planning for remote projects is to identify potential risks. This could include technical issues, communication breakdowns, or delays in deliverables. By conducting a thorough risk assessment, project managers can better understand the potential threats to their projects and develop appropriate responses.

Once risks have been identified, project managers can then develop contingency plans to address them. This could involve having backup communication channels in place, setting up regular check-ins with team members, or creating alternative timelines for key deliverables. By having these plans in place, project managers can respond quickly and effectively to any unforeseen challenges that may arise.

In addition to developing contingency plans, project managers should also regularly review and update them as needed. As remote projects evolve, new risks may emerge, requiring adjustments to existing plans. By staying proactive and flexible, project managers can better position themselves to handle whatever comes their way. Overall, contingency planning is a crucial aspect of successful remote project management. By anticipating potential risks, developing response strategies, and staying proactive, project managers can ensure that their projects run smoothly, even in the face of uncertainty.

Chapter 6: Monitoring and Evaluating Remote Projects

Tracking Progress in Remote Projects

In the world of remote project management, tracking progress is essential to ensure that projects are on schedule and within budget. With team members scattered across different locations and time zones, it can be challenging to keep tabs on everyone's tasks and milestones. However, with the right tools and techniques, project managers can effectively monitor progress and make adjustments as needed.

One of the most important tools for tracking progress in remote projects is project management software. These platforms allow project managers to create detailed project plans, assign tasks to team members, and track progress in real-time. By using project management software, project managers can easily see which tasks are on track and which ones are falling behind, allowing them to take proactive measures to keep the project on schedule.

In addition to project management software, regular check-ins with team members are crucial for tracking progress in remote projects. These check-ins can take the form of virtual meetings, email updates, or even phone calls. By staying in constant communication with team members, project managers can get a better sense of where things stand and address any issues before they escalate.

Another important aspect of tracking progress in remote projects is setting clear milestones and deadlines. By breaking down the project into smaller tasks and setting deadlines for each one, project managers can easily track progress and ensure that the project stays on track. Additionally, setting milestones allows project managers to celebrate small victories along the way, boosting team morale and motivation.

Overall, tracking progress in remote projects requires a combination of tools, techniques, and effective communication. By using project management software, staying in regular communication with team members, and setting clear milestones, project managers can effectively monitor progress and ensure the success of their remote projects.

Evaluating Remote Team Performance

As a project or programme manager, evaluating remote team performance can be a challenging task. With team members spread across different locations and time zones, it can be difficult to track progress, communicate effectively, and ensure that everyone is working towards the same goals. However, by implementing the right tools and strategies, you can effectively evaluate and improve the performance of your remote team.

One of the most important aspects of evaluating remote team performance is setting clear expectations from the outset. Clearly define project goals, deadlines, and deliverables so that team members know exactly what is expected of them. Regular communication is also key - schedule regular check-ins, team meetings, and one-on-one discussions to keep everyone on the same page and address any issues or concerns that may arise.

Utilizing project management software can also greatly improve your ability to evaluate team performance. Tools such as Trello,

Asana, or Monday.com can help you track progress, assign tasks, and monitor deadlines in real-time. These tools allow you to see who is working on what, how far along they are, and where any potential bottlenecks may be occurring.

In addition to setting clear expectations and utilizing project management tools, it's important to provide regular feedback to your remote team. Recognize and reward achievements, provide constructive criticism when necessary, and offer support and guidance to help team members succeed. By fostering a culture of open communication and continuous improvement, you can ensure that your remote team is performing at their best.

Overall, evaluating remote team performance requires a combination of clear expectations, effective communication, project management tools, and regular feedback. By implementing these strategies, you can effectively evaluate and improve the performance of your remote team, leading to greater success for your projects and programmes.

Reporting on Remote Project Success

Reporting on remote project success is crucial for project managers and programme managers to showcase the effectiveness of their management strategies and the successful outcomes of their projects. In the realm of remote project management, where team members are scattered across different locations and time zones, it is even more important to provide clear and concise reports that highlight key achievements, challenges, and lessons learned.

One of the key aspects of reporting on remote project success is to focus on measurable outcomes. This could include meeting project deadlines, staying within budget, achieving desired project objectives, and delivering high-quality results. By quantifying these achievements, project managers can demonstrate the value of their management efforts and the effectiveness of their remote project management strategies.

Another important element of reporting on remote project success is to communicate effectively with stakeholders. This includes providing regular updates on the progress of the project, addressing any concerns or issues that may arise, and seeking feedback from team members and clients. By keeping stakeholders informed and engaged, project managers can build trust and confidence in their ability to successfully manage remote projects.

In addition to highlighting successes, it is also important to address any challenges or obstacles that were encountered during the project. This could include issues related to communication, collaboration, technology, or cultural differences. By acknowledging these challenges and sharing the strategies used to overcome them, project managers can demonstrate their resilience and adaptability in managing remote projects.

Ultimately, reporting on remote project success is about showcasing the achievements, lessons learned, and best practices that can be applied to future projects. By providing clear and comprehensive reports, project managers can inspire confidence in their management abilities and drive success in their remote project management endeavors.

Chapter 7: Remote Project Closure and Lessons Learned

Closing Out Remote Projects

Closing out remote projects is a crucial step in the project management process. It involves completing all remaining tasks, documenting lessons learned, and ensuring that the project is officially closed and all resources are released.

One key aspect of closing out remote projects is conducting a thorough project review. This involves evaluating the project's success, identifying areas for improvement, and documenting lessons learned. By reflecting on what went well and what could have been done better, project managers can improve their remote project management skills and strategies for future projects.

Another important step in closing out remote projects is ensuring that all project deliverables have been completed and approved by stakeholders. This includes finalizing any outstanding tasks, obtaining sign-offs on project documentation, and ensuring that all project objectives have been met.

Additionally, project managers should ensure that all resources, including team members, equipment, and budget, are properly released and accounted for. This helps to close out the project in an organized and efficient manner, while also allowing team members to move on to their next assignments.

Overall, closing out remote projects requires attention to detail, effective communication with stakeholders, and a commitment to continuous improvement. By following these guidelines and best practices, project managers can ensure that their remote projects are completed successfully and that lessons learned are applied to future projects.

Conducting Post-Project Reviews

After successfully completing a remote project, it is crucial for project managers and programme managers to conduct post-project reviews to assess the project's overall success and identify areas for improvement in future projects. These reviews play a vital role in continuous improvement and help in achieving better project outcomes in the future.

The first step in conducting a post-project review is to gather feedback from the project team members, stakeholders, and clients. This feedback can provide valuable insights into what worked well during the project and what could have been done differently. It is important to create a safe and open environment where team members feel comfortable sharing their honest opinions and suggestions.

During the review, project managers should analyze the project's performance against the initial objectives, budget, timeline, and quality standards. They should also identify any challenges or roadblocks that were encountered during the project and discuss how they were resolved. By evaluating these factors, project managers can identify areas where improvements can be made for future projects.

In addition to evaluating the project's performance, project managers should also assess their own performance as well as the performance of the project team. This self-assessment can help in identifying areas where leadership skills can be improved and where additional training or support may be needed for team members.

Overall, conducting post-project reviews is essential for remote project managers and programme managers to learn from past experiences, improve their project management skills, and ensure successful outcomes in future projects. By taking the time to reflect on what went well and what could have been done better, project managers can continue to grow and excel in their roles.

Implementing Lessons Learned for Future Remote Projects

As project managers and programme managers in the realm of remote project management, it is crucial to continuously learn and adapt in order to achieve success in our projects. One of the most effective ways to improve our remote project management skills is by implementing lessons learned from past projects into future endeavors.

One key aspect of implementing lessons learned for future remote projects is to conduct a thorough post-project review. This involves gathering feedback from team members, stakeholders, and other key individuals involved in the project to identify what went well and what could have been improved. By analyzing the successes and challenges of past projects, we can gain valuable insights that can be applied to future projects.

Another important step in implementing lessons learned for future remote projects is to create a repository of best practices and lessons learned. This can include documenting successful project management strategies, communication techniques, and problem-solving approaches that have proven to be effective in remote project environments. By creating a centralized repository of lessons learned, project managers can easily access this valuable information and apply it to future projects.

Furthermore, it is essential to communicate and share lessons learned with other project managers and team members. By sharing experiences and insights from past projects, we can foster a culture of continuous learning and improvement within our remote project management teams. This open communication not only helps us learn from each other's experiences but also encourages collaboration and innovation in our projects.

In conclusion, implementing lessons learned for future remote projects is a critical component of effective project management. By conducting post-project reviews, creating a repository of best practices, and fostering a culture of sharing and learning, project managers can enhance their remote project management skills and achieve greater success in their projects.

Chapter 8: Remote Project Manager's Toolbox

Resource Management Tools

Resource Management Tools are essential for remote project managers to effectively plan, allocate, and track resources for successful project delivery. In this subchapter, we will explore some of the top tools available to help you manage your resources efficiently and maximize productivity in remote project management.

One of the most popular resource management tools is Trello, a user-friendly project management software that allows you to create boards, lists, and cards to organize tasks and resources. With Trello, project managers can easily assign tasks to team members, set deadlines, and track progress in real-time, all in one centralized platform.

Another valuable resource management tool is Asana, a versatile project management software that enables project managers to create tasks, set priorities, and collaborate with team members on projects. With Asana, remote project managers can effectively allocate resources, track progress, and communicate with team members, ensuring that everyone is on the same page and working towards a common goal.

For more advanced resource management needs, project managers can turn to tools like Microsoft Project, a comprehensive project management software that offers a wide range of features for planning, scheduling, and tracking resources. With Microsoft Project, project managers can create detailed project plans, allocate resources efficiently, and monitor progress to ensure that projects are completed on time and within budget.

Overall, resource management tools play a crucial role in remote project management, helping project managers effectively plan, allocate, and track resources to ensure successful project delivery. By utilizing these tools, project managers can streamline their workflows, improve collaboration with team members, and ultimately achieve project success.

Budgeting Tools for Remote Projects

Budgeting for remote projects can present unique challenges for project managers. With team members located in different regions or even countries, it can be difficult to accurately track expenses and allocate resources effectively. Fortunately, there are a variety of budgeting tools available to help remote project managers stay on top of their finances and ensure the success of their projects.

One popular budgeting tool for remote projects is cloud-based project management software. These platforms allow project managers to create detailed budgets, track expenses in real-time, and generate reports to analyze spending patterns. With features like automated invoicing and expense tracking, project managers can easily monitor their budget and make adjustments as needed. Another useful budgeting tool for remote projects is online collaboration tools. These platforms allow team members to communicate and share documents in real-time, making it easier to collaborate on budgeting tasks. By using these tools, project managers can ensure that everyone is on the same page when it comes to budgeting and that important information is easily accessible to all team members.

In addition to software tools, project managers can also benefit from using financial management apps to track expenses and manage budgets on-the-go. These apps can sync with bank accounts and credit cards, making it easy to monitor spending and stay within budget limits. By leveraging these tools, project managers can ensure that their remote projects stay on track financially and achieve success.

Overall, budgeting for remote projects requires a combination of effective communication, collaboration, and the right tools. By utilizing cloud-based project management software, online collaboration tools, and financial management apps, project managers can effectively manage their budgets and ensure the success of their remote projects.

Remote Project Documentation and Reporting

In the world of remote project management, effective documentation and reporting play a crucial role in ensuring the success of a project. Without clear and concise documentation, team members may become confused about project goals, tasks, and deadlines. This can lead to miscommunication, missed deadlines, and ultimately, project failure.

To address this challenge, remote project managers must establish a robust system for documenting project details and progress. This system should include guidelines for creating and maintaining project documentation, as well as tools for organizing and sharing this information with team members.

One key aspect of remote project documentation is the use of online project management tools. These tools allow team members to collaborate on documents in real-time, track project progress, and communicate effectively with one another. Popular project management tools such as Trello, Asana, and Jira offer features that make it easy to create and maintain project documentation, even when team members are spread out across different locations.

In addition to using online tools, remote project managers should also establish regular reporting procedures to keep stakeholders informed about project progress. This may include weekly status updates, monthly progress reports, or ad-hoc reports as needed. By providing stakeholders with timely and accurate information about project status, remote project managers can build trust and confidence in their ability to successfully manage the project.

Overall, effective project documentation and reporting are essential components of successful remote project management. By establishing clear guidelines, using online tools, and providing regular updates to stakeholders, project managers can ensure that their projects stay on track and meet their goals, even in a remote work environment.

Chapter 9: Developing Remote Project Management Skills

Continuous Learning in Remote Project Management

Continuous learning is essential for project managers, especially those working in a remote setting. In the fast-paced world of project management, staying up-to-date with the latest tools, techniques, and best practices is crucial for ensuring the success of your projects. This subchapter will explore the importance of continuous learning in remote project management and provide practical tips for staying ahead of the curve.

One of the key benefits of continuous learning in remote project management is that it allows you to adapt to the ever-changing landscape of the industry. By staying informed about new trends and developments, you can better anticipate challenges and proactively address them before they become major issues. This proactive approach can help you avoid costly delays and keep your projects on track.

Continuous learning also helps you stay competitive in the job market. As technology continues to evolve, project managers who are able to leverage the latest tools and techniques are in high demand. By investing in your professional development, you can position yourself as a valuable asset to your organization and enhance your career prospects.

In this subchapter, we will explore various ways to incorporate continuous learning into your remote project management practice. From attending industry conferences and workshops to enrolling in online courses and certifications, there are plenty of opportunities to expand your knowledge and skills. We will also discuss the importance of networking with other project managers and seeking mentorship from experienced professionals in the field.

By making continuous learning a priority in your remote project management practice, you can enhance your expertise, advance your career, and ultimately, deliver more successful projects. Stay tuned for practical tips and strategies for incorporating continuous learning into your daily routine.

Building Leadership Skills for Remote Projects

In today's fast-paced and ever-changing business landscape, remote project management has become increasingly common. Project Managers and Programme Managers are often tasked with leading teams spread across different locations, time zones, and even countries. This presents unique challenges that require a specific set of leadership skills to effectively manage remote projects.

Building leadership skills for remote projects starts with effective communication. Clear and consistent communication is key to keeping remote teams aligned and motivated. Utilizing various communication tools such as video conferencing, instant messaging, and project management software can help facilitate regular communication and collaboration among team members.

Another important leadership skill for remote projects is the ability to inspire and motivate team members. Remote team members may feel isolated or disconnected from the rest of the team, so it's important for project managers to create a sense of camaraderie and teamwork. Encouraging open communication, recognizing individual achievements, and fostering a supportive team culture can help boost morale and productivity.

Adaptability is also crucial for remote project managers. They must be able to quickly adjust to changing circumstances, anticipate potential issues, and find creative solutions to overcome challenges. This requires flexibility, problem-solving skills, and the ability to think on your feet.

Finally, building trust among team members is essential for successful remote project management. Trust is the foundation of any successful team, and remote teams are no exception. Project managers must demonstrate trustworthiness, transparency, and reliability to build strong relationships with team members.

By honing these leadership skills, Project Managers and Programme Managers can effectively navigate the complexities of remote projects and lead their teams to success. With the right tools and techniques, remote project management can be made easy, efficient, and rewarding for everyone involved.

Adapting to Changing Remote Work Environments

In today's fast-paced and ever-changing business landscape, project managers and programme managers must be able to adapt to shifting remote work environments. The ability to effectively manage remote teams and projects is essential for success in the modern workplace. This subchapter will provide valuable insights and tools for project managers looking to navigate the challenges of remote work and ensure the success of their projects.

One of the key aspects of adapting to changing remote work environments is maintaining open and effective communication with team members. With team members spread out across different locations, it is crucial to establish clear channels of communication and set expectations for how and when team members will communicate. Utilizing tools such as video conferencing, messaging platforms, and project management software can help keep everyone on the same page and ensure that work is getting done efficiently. Another important aspect of adapting to changing remote work environments is being flexible and open to new ways of working. As project managers, it is essential to be willing to try new approaches and technologies to meet the needs of remote teams. This may involve experimenting with different project management methodologies, adjusting timelines and deliverables, or finding creative ways to foster team collaboration and engagement.
By embracing flexibility, communication, and innovation, project managers can successfully adapt to changing remote work environments and ensure the success of their projects. The Remote Project Manager's Handbook provides valuable tools and strategies for navigating the complexities of remote project management, making it easier for project managers to thrive in today's remote work environment.

Chapter 10: Conclusion

Summary of Key Points

The "Summary of Key Points" section in "The Remote Project Manager's Handbook: Tools for Effective Management" serves as a comprehensive overview of the essential takeaways covered in the book. Aimed at project and program managers looking to navigate the complexities of remote project management with ease, this summary distills the most important concepts for quick reference and application.

Key points highlighted in this section include the importance of clear communication in remote project management, the value of leveraging technology and tools to facilitate collaboration, and the significance of establishing trust and building strong relationships with remote team members. Additionally, the summary emphasizes the need for effective time management, efficient task delegation, and proactive problem-solving strategies to ensure project success. Furthermore, the summary delves into the significance of setting clear goals and expectations, providing regular feedback and support to team members, and fostering a positive team culture in a remote work environment. It also touches upon the importance of adaptability, flexibility, and resilience in the face of unexpected challenges and changes.

Overall, the "Summary of Key Points" section in "The Remote Project Manager's Handbook" offers a concise and practical guide for project and program managers seeking to enhance their remote management skills. By focusing on these key points, readers can better understand the fundamental principles and strategies necessary for effective remote project management and apply them to their own projects with confidence and success.

Final Thoughts on Remote Project Management Success

In conclusion, remote project management success is achievable with the right tools, strategies, and mindset. As project managers and programme managers in the niche of remote project management, it is crucial to understand the unique challenges and opportunities that come with leading virtual teams.

One key takeaway is the importance of effective communication. Clear and consistent communication is essential to keep remote teams aligned and informed. Utilize various communication tools such as video conferencing, instant messaging, and project management software to stay connected with team members and stakeholders.

Another critical factor for success is building trust within your virtual team. Trust is the foundation of any successful project, and it becomes even more crucial in a remote setting where face-to-face interactions are limited. Encourage open and honest communication, set clear expectations, and empower team members to take ownership of their responsibilities.

Additionally, it is essential to establish a structured workflow and project management process. Define roles and responsibilities, set deadlines and milestones, and create a transparent project plan that everyone can access and reference. This will help keep the project on track and ensure that everyone is working towards the same goals.

Finally, don't forget to celebrate successes and learn from failures. Acknowledge the hard work and achievements of your remote team members, and use setbacks as opportunities for growth and improvement. By fostering a positive and collaborative team environment, you can overcome any challenges that come your way and achieve success in remote project management.

In conclusion, remote project management success is within reach for project managers and programme managers in the niche of remote project management made easy. By implementing the right strategies, tools, and mindset, you can lead your virtual team to success and deliver outstanding results.